I0430205

CONTENTS

Foundations of Defense Transformation

Why Transform The Military?

The future is unknowable. But that is no excuse for inaction. A more prudent course is to experiment, develop diverse and sometimes competing operational concepts, make the necessary preliminary investments, then play out the options.

-National Defense Panel

It can be argued the United States military is the greatest force ever to walk the face of the Earth. Yet, the strategic environment of today is characterized by an uncertainty greater than during any point in our history. The psyche of America changed after the terrorist attack on 11 September 2001.

The Pentagon, September 11.

At this point, President Bush was forced to reconsider the Nation's military and strategic needs. The President's new strategy called for a more aggressive approach to the use of force against regimes planning to attack the United States. The new policy stated America would act unilaterally if it had warning of an impending attack. This new policy also modified the forward deployment posture of U.S. Armed Forces. In the past, U.S. forces were forward deployed to contain conflicts and reassure both allies and potential enemies that the United States was committed to being involved. Now, U.S. forces will be forward deployed to be ready to engage an enemy at a moment's notice if necessary. If U.S. forces are to be primed and ready to engage potential adversaries based on warnings alone, then they must transform their strategic warning and surveillance systems, develop a long range strike capability, and expand the Nation's stockpile of precision conventional munitions for use against enemy biological, chemical, and nuclear weapons.

The military does not know when it will face another major challenge to its security, who might pose such a challenge, or how the challenger would chose to compete.[1] Historical patterns over the last three hundred years strongly suggest that competition among the great powers is the rule, rather than the exception.[2] The United States' seeming monopoly on precision guided weapons, stealth technology, and space will not endure beyond the next decade. Technology diffusion will allow future adversaries to present the U.S. military with new, and far more difficult problems to solve than those encountered during the Gulf War.[3] Sweden, for example, is a nation that is transforming its military and dealing with how technology diffusion might impact our national security.

---

[1] Andrew Krepinevich, "Transforming the American Military", *Backgrounder*, 26 September 1997, 1.
[2] Ibid, 1.
[3] Ibid. 2.

The Swedes have determined any future threat to their nation will most likely happen across the Baltic.[4] So they're rethinking the technology needed to defend a nation bordered by sea frontiers. It's possible they will make some innovation that another nation might capitalize on. For example, they've designed three new naval vessels. One is an air independent submarine running on fuel cells rather than nuclear power, which allows it to travel almost silently and remain submerged for extended periods of time. They have a surface ship that's a bit more conventional and a radically new designed naval vessel called the Visby which has practically no metal other than the engine.[5] It's constructed to be stealthy. Exportation of this technology to a peer competitor could have an impact to our national security. The current administration wants to enhance the military's force structure to address these potential threats.

Sticking with the current force structure doesn't make sense. In fact, sticking with this current force structure may reduce our ability to face future foes. Threats to our national security in the foreseeable future will be quite different from those in the last half of the 20th century for which our current force structure was designed to defeat.

The lack of a peer competitor places the United States in the enviable position of unquestioned military superiority worldwide. This disproportionality creates an asymmetric advantage every adversary must contend with. As competitors develop new battlefield techniques and technologies, it is imperative we continue developing new weapon systems and schemes of maneuver. It is time for the United States to take the next evolutionary step in securing the viability of the American armed forces. The

---

[4] Kingdom of Sweden, *Annual Exchange of Information on Defense Planning*, Vienna Document 1999, 3.
[5] Ibid, 13.

2001 Quadrennial Defense Review (QDR) lays the foundation for this evolutionary

change.

Quadrennial Defense Review

In defining the defense priorities for the United States, the President stated he

wanted the U.S. to maintain its leadership role in the world; fight and win the war on

terror; and defend the American people from a range of potential treats: asymmetric,

ballistic, and cruise missiles. [6]

The 2001 QDR translated the President's guidance into defense policy by shifting the basis of

defense planning from a threat-based model to a capabilities-based model focused on how an

opponent might fight rather than specifically whom the adversary might be or where the fight

might occur. The defense strategy, as articulated by the QDR, seeks to prepare the military for a

future by focusing on six operational goals. The six operational goals for transforming the

military into a capabilities-based force are as follows: protecting critical bases of operation

including the homeland; denying enemies sanctuary through persistent surveillance, tracking,

and rapid engagement with high volume precision strikes; projecting and sustaining force in

distant denied areas; leveraging information technology and innovative concepts in a joint

manner; conducting effective information operations; and enhancing the capability and

survivability of space systems and supporting infrastructure.[7] Effective integration is the key to

success.

---

[6] President George W. Bush, speech presented at the National Defense University, Washington, DC, 2001.
[7] Department of Defense, *Quadrennial Defense Review Report*, 30 September 2001, 30. Cited herafter as 2001 QDR.

The QDR emphasizes adapting existing military capabilities along with exploiting new military technologies as a means of meeting the challenges of the future. The principal challenge before the United States military is not to be found in its ability to fight and win two nearly simultaneous major regional conflicts of the magnitude and type of Desert Storm. Rather, it is in the military's ability to extend its current advantage in military effectiveness in a world rapidly changing and far more formidable. This would contribute to an U.S. national security strategy whose principal goal is to avoid another cycle of military competition.[8]

The QDR states transforming America's defense for the 21st century will require a longstanding commitment from our country and its leaders. Transformation is not a goal for tomorrow, but an endeavor that must be embraced in earnest today.[9]

TRANSFORMATION

"The goal is not to transform the entire military in one year, or even in one decade. That would be both unnecessary and unwise. Transformation is a process, and, because the world is not static, it is a process that must continue. In short, there will be no point where our forces will have been "transformed." Rather, we aim to transform between 5-10% of the force, turning it into the leading edge of change that will, over time, continue to lead the rest of the force into the 21st century. We cannot know today precisely where transformation will take us. It is a process that will unfold over time…".

-Secretary of Defense, Donald H. Rumsfeld
2 February 2002, HAC/D Posture Hearing

Transformation is a process for bridging today's force structure to what you believe you will need in the future to employ new concepts of operation. As such, they are evolutionary in nature and can include one or all of the following: new technologies; new operational schemes; and/or new institutional reforms (see Table 1). The Air Force

---

[8] Krepinevich, 2.
[9] 2001 QDR, IV.

views transformation as just a means to a desired end state. Today that desired end state includes the following: creating a totally integrated combined arms force, horizontally integrated across functions, and focused on effects based operations.

Transformation Is	Transformation Is Not
A sustained, dynamic process	A defined or unchanging blueprint
Integrating new concepts, processes, technologies, and organizational designs that make previous approaches obsolete or less effective	A silver bullet
Rebalancing existing capabilities or leveraging old technologies in new ways Substantial improvements in how we currently perform and Entirely new ways of conducting war	Something done to all the force at once
Seeking to maintain a substantial margin of advantage over potential adversaries, minimize opportunity for surprise, and mitigate the effects of surprise	Accomplished in a short period of time
	Just about systems or platforms

Table 1. The Transformation Concept

One clear example of a successful transformation was the introduction of the airplane. Most pioneers of aviation didn't see in 1920 just how the transformation of this new technology would play out. Brigadier General William "Billy" Mitchell thought strategic aviation would make both armies and navies obsolete. Other pioneers thought large airships were the wave of the future. Some naval aviation pioneers believed in seaplanes while others developed the carrier concept. Aviation penetrated every area of warfare and led to several new operational concepts: air transportation, airborne troops, gliders, strategic bombers, scouting, anti-submarine warfare, ground support, and air superiority.

Conflicting definitions have confused the meaning and purpose of transformation. In general, theories of transformation fall into two schools of thought. The first links transformation exclusively with the term revolution in military affairs (RMA). An RMA is widely described as an order-of-magnitude change in the way the military conducts warfare that renders the status quo obsolete. RMAs combine new evolutionary or revolutionary technology with organizational and conceptual changes that maximize the effectiveness and potential of that technology. Secretary of Defense Rumsfeld's vision of transformation falls under this school of thought. Followers of this view use the terms transformation and RMA interchangeably.

Historically, innovations have preceded transformations and transformations have preceded RMAs. An innovation reflects any level of new equipment or application, from field radios to advance tactical fighter aircraft or new idea from an organization.[10]

The other school of thought views transformation simply as a means of changing the U.S. military from a Cold War force to a post-Cold War military prepared to meet the challenges of a new security environment. Under this approach, transformational efforts enable the United States to deal with new security environments through evolutionary means vice revolutionary as with the RMA school. [11]

Service transformation plans reflect both views (see Table 2). In some instances, affecting a military transformation will mean greater competition among the military

---

[10] William B. Scott, "Innovation Is Currency of USAF Space Battlelab," *Aviation Week and Space Technology*, 3 April 2000, 52-53.
[11] HQ USAF/XPXT, *The USAF Transformation Flight Plan FY03-07*, 2002. 2.

services. Congress and many military reformers have decried the amount of overlap and redundancy that exists among the four military services. However, competition among the Services can also assist in determining how best to exploit new capabilities, or how to solve emerging challenges.

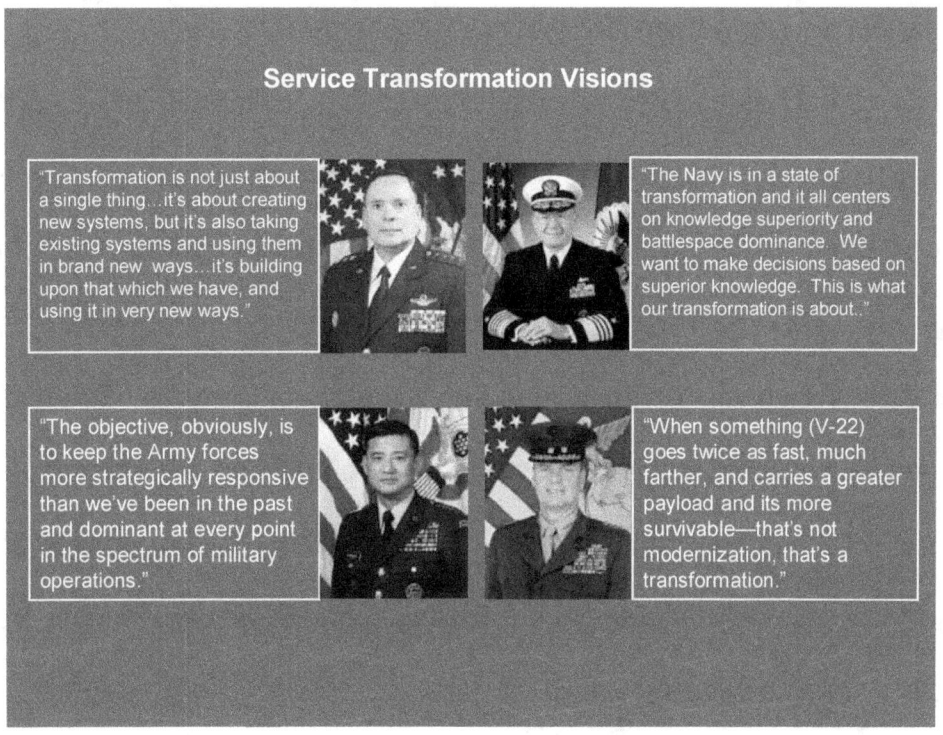

Table 2. Service Transformation Visions

This kind of competition should be encouraged. Allocating a new mission to one military service runs the risk of falling into the trap of false efficiencies. In the case of the anti-access challenge, for example, it is not yet clear whether the solution is to be found in Air Force long-range precision strikes, strikes from a Navy task force comprising a "distributed" capital ship (i.e., carriers, and arsenal ships and Trident "stealth battleships" fitted with hundreds of vertical launch systems for long-range precision guided munitions, all linked by an expanded version of the Navy's Cooperative Engagement Capability battle-management network and Marine "infestation" forces), Army forces employing long range missiles, or weaponized unmanned aerial vehicles (UAVs), or a combination of these capabilities, or perhaps something quite different.[12] It is the role of civilian leadership within the Department of Defense to sort these issues.

The Air Force defines transformation as a process by which the military achieves and maintains asymmetric advantage through changes in operational concepts, organizational structure, and/or technologies that significantly improve warfighting capabilities or the ability to meet the demands of a changing security environment.[13] This definition is in line with the thinking of the Secretary of Defense. To bring the Air Force in compliance with the QDR, its acquisition priorities and transformational goals were focused on acquiring weapon systems which fulfill the QDR's requirement to procure systems capable of meeting the following capabilities: persistent surveillance, precision strike, and power projection.

Technologies Driving Air Force Transformation

A central objective of the 2001 QDR was to shift the basis of defense planning from treat based model that has dominated thinking in the past to a capabilities based model squarely focused on the future The capabilities based model focuses more on how an adversary might fight rather than specifically whom the adversary might be or where a

---

[12] Krepinevich, 7.
[13] USAF Transformation Flight Plan FY03-07, pg 5

war might occur.[14] This strategy seeks to create a broad portfolio of military capabilities to increase strategic opportunities and decrease the potential for strategic surprise. The systems listed below provide capabilities supporting the operational goals of the QDR.

In most cases of peacetime military innovation, technological developments played an enabling role in creating new ways of fighting. In a narrow and specific sense, such innovative developments were revolutionary. Yet, the underlying technologies themselves (the internal combustion engine, radio communications, etc.), as well as the new military systems to which they gave birth (airplanes, tanks, amphibious landing craft, aircraft carriers, and so forth), formed only a part of these innovations, if not the smallest part.[15]

The Air Force is answering OSD's call for transformational technologies by bringing three new capabilities to the joint fight: F/A-22 Raptor, Small Diameter Bomb (SDB), and the Spaced Based Radar (SBR). These acquisition priorities represent what the Air Force believes it will need in the future to be successful: persistent surveillance, precision munitions, and a long-range strike capability. Each capability represents a requirement the 2001 QDR asked services to fill.

---

[14] QDR, IV.

[15] William Murray and Allan R. Millett, *Military Innovation in the Interwar Period*, (New York, NY: Cambridge University Press, 1996), 371.

F/A-22 Raptor

The F-22 was conceived during the Cold War as an air superiority replacement for the F-15. It was renamed the F/A-22 after the acquisition started to run into flak within OSD to emphasize the addition of air-to-ground functions. Along with a new designation, the F-22 was recast as a strategic imperative in protecting not only the United States but its allies throughout the world.

For the past decade, many military analysts have argued that the combination of a drawdown in overseas bases and increased worldwide commitments have necessitated added emphasis on power projection and a long-range strike capability. This requirement has been underlined by access concerns in which remaining overseas bases are increasingly vulnerable to missile attacks, terrorism, and weapons of mass destruction. At the same time, it is feared these bases will become more vulnerable to political pressure from countries in the region. The F/A-22 is being billed as a bridge to addressing these problems. It will be assigned the QDR responsibilities of protecting critical bases of operations, delivering high volume precision strikes, power projection, and leveraging information technology in new and creative ways.

It is a leap-ahead technology and transformational in every sense of the word. The F/A-22's combination of stealth, supercruise (the ability to sustain supersonic flight without the use of gas guzzling afterburners), maneuverability, integrated avionics, and ability to gather intelligence on enemy intentions separates it from legacy fighters and giving it unprecedented capabilities over other systems.

All current aircraft suffer from the same disadvantages: while they can fight in smaller numbers to create precise or even mass effects, they must be employed in a package to be survivable against sophisticated air defense threat arrays. Current air operations in the enemy's territory are a sequence of missions executed to try to suppress or kill an enemy airplane or SAMs in order to allow attack aircraft or ground units to maneuver. The Raptor allows combatant commanders to take the fight to the enemy from the opening minute of the campaign. Its advanced avionics will extend the reconnaissance network over the battlefield providing considerable information about an adversary's location and actions.

Although the F/A-22 represents a transformational technology, its acquisition will not come without a cost. The aircraft is extremely expensive and there are much cheaper alternatives in the form of heavy bombers, long-range unmanned vehicles, and life extension programs for the F-15 are available. Ultimately, any dollars used to procure the F/A-22 could be used to develop these alternative technologies.

Small Diameter Bomb

The science behind the SDB represents the biggest development in munitions since World War II.[16] As with the technical revolutions in the First World War, chemistry and physics are driving many of the advances of today in weapons  development. Forty years of research has yielded ways to manipulate explosives at the molecular level making them exponentially better. It's fair to say, researchers at Lawrence Livermore Laboratories and scientist at the Eglin Air Force Base through combining breakthrough computer simulation codes and state-of-the-art diagnostics have taken the science of creating high explosives to a new level.

The SDB is a 250 pound weapon with the same penetration capabilities as a 2000 pound bomb, but with only 50 pounds of explosive. One variant of the bomb is equipped with an INS/GPS guidance system suitable for fixed and stationary targets. A second variant adds automatic target recognition to seek and destroy mobile and relocatable targets. The warhead is designed to maximize penetration without sacrificing

---

[16] Randall Simpson. Transforming Explosive Art into Science. www.llnl.gov/Simpson.html, 4.

blast/fragmentation potential. [17]

The SDB is considered one of the most significant programs on the books because it will dramatically increase the strike capability of every combat aircraft in the inventory. It will increase the number of kills per pass and increase weapons loadout thereby minimizing the number of combat forces needed to achieve operational objectives early in a conflict. In the case of the F/A-22, it will permit the destruction of up to eight targets in a single mission.

Without question, the SDB represents a transformational technology. It is evolutionary if not revolutionary, in that previous methods of creating munitions are now obsolete. By dramatically increasing the strike capability of every combat aircraft in the inventory, it will bring a degree of mass never seen before on the battlefield. It is an absolutely perfect fit for the QDR's call for the development of high volume precision strike weapons.

Space Based Radar

SBR will provide much improved battlefield intelligence. The goal is to achieve an initial SBR capability by 2010. One of the greatest benefits is that SBR will give U.S. forces Ground Moving Target Indicator data day or night, in any weather.. Desert Storm highlighted the need for on-demand, persistent surveillance to track and kill elusive mobile ground targets. SBR's real value stems from the fact it can look down, unobstructed by mountainous terrain, heavy foliage or bad weather and provide a

---

[17] HQ ACC/DR, *CAF Operational Requirements Document for Miniature Munitions and Carriage System*, 1-5.

dynamic electronic view of the battlefield. An enemy cannot hide behind obscuring

terrain features to avoid detection. Furthermore, it will also be able to look deeper into

enemy territory than would be possible with Joint STARS (Surveillance, Targeting, and

Attack Radar System). SBR would not put aircrew members or unmanned vehicles at

risk and it would be available in wartime or peacetime. SBR data will fuse data

collected by Joint STARS, AWACS (Airborne Warning and Control Systems),

unmanned aerial vehicles, and other platforms to present a coherent picture of an area

to field commanders. The Air Force wants SBR data to be linked directly into cockpits,

tactical vehicles on the ground, and ship command centers, as well as to stateside

intelligence analysis hubs.[18]

It's not clear whether SBR will become a transformational technology because its

final architecture is still in question. SBR and other information technology systems

utilize a concept of attack that comes from John Boyd's strategic paralysis theory. As

Colonel David Fadock succinctly described Boyd's theory in the *Path of Heaven: The*

Evolution of Airpower: the aim of warfare is to "render the enemy powerless by denying

him the time to cope mentally."[19]

Information technology seeks to change the nature of warfare. "The Clausewitzian

thoughts on the nature of war, the relationships between policy and use of military

power, and the effect of fog of war, and friction are tossed away as unimportant in the

information age."[20] History has shown, however, that the nature of warfare is

---

[18] John A Tirpak, "The Spaced Based Radar Plan," *Air Force Magazine*, August 2002, 1.
[19] Colonel Philip S. Melinger, *The Path of Heaven: The Evolution of Airpower Theory*, 357-389
[20] Ibid., 2.

immutable.

The proponents of information technology acknowledge that although the friction and fog of war may have existed in the past, it was caused by a lack of battlespace awareness and not by the immutable nature of war. They assert that a vast array of sensors and computers netted together will reduce friction and fog to manageable levels. The uncertainties, upon which a commander's decisions are based, however, can never be fully mastered, regardless of advances in information technologies. Friction and fog of war, chance and luck, all make any war highly unpredictable and full of unforeseen events.[21]

Dr. Milan Vego, a professor of operations at the Naval War College, writing in the U.S. Naval Institute Proceedings, challenged many of information warfare principles. "The U.S. military is well on its way to eliminating the distinctions between the art of war and military science, because of its obsession with new technologies," Vego continues: "As explained by its leading proponents, Network Centric Warfare bears a striking resemblance to various discarded theories of war fashionable over the last two centuries. Experience shows that information superiority does not guarantee sound decisions or ultimate victory. Although increasingly critical, information is just one of many factors in the commander's success in combat. Timely and relevant information is of little value if war is conducted with an unsound and incoherent strategy and poor application of operational art or tactics."[22]

---

[21] Ibib., 2.
[22] Ibid., 3.

REVOLUTION IN MILITARY AFFAIRS

According to Andrew Marshal, director of the Office of Net Assessments in the Office of the Secretary of Defense, "a Revolution in Military Affairs (RMA) is a major change in the nature of warfare brought about by the innovative application of new technologies which, combined with dramatic changes in military doctrine and operational and organizational concepts, fundamentally alters the character and conduct of military operations." The nature of these discontinuities is such that warfare after the revolution is unlike what went on before in profound and significant ways.[23] Many believe the United States is in the mid-stages of a third revolution in military affairs for the 20th century. The key attributes of this RMA include increasing reliance on precision systems, improved information exploitation, increased communication availability, and rapid advancement in predictive methods and materials science. The post-Gulf War period has seen a coalescence of military-technical revolution theory in a high-tech approach to war.

Interwar Period

---

[23] Barry R. Schneider and Lawrence E. Grinter, *Battlefield of the Future: 21st Century Warfare Issues* (Maxwell Air Force Base, AL: Air University Press, 1998), 65.

The 20th Century has witnessed two periods of military revolution. Both periods of change took place during times of peace and within an atmosphere of ambiguity. Senior leaders and planners didn't know who they would fight next or when that conflict would be beginning. The first revolution took place during the 1920s and 1930s where a transformation in land warfare and maneuver culminated with the Germans developing the blitzkrieg concept. Also during this period, naval aviators convinced their service to transform and create carrier battle groups. The second occurred between the 1940s and 1950s where nuclear weapons were developed and placed on ballistic missiles and strategic bombers.

"The emerging strategic environment in which our military institutions will have to operate suggests a number of similarities to the period between the great world wars of the first half of this century. During this timeframe, military institutions had to come to grips with enormous technological and tactical innovations during a period of minimal funding and low resource support. Some succeeded, creating a huge impact on the opening moves in World War II. Others were less successful and some institutional innovation resulted in dismal military failure."[24]

Blitzkrieg

The Treaty of Versailles imposed draconian terms of surrender on the Germans following its defeat in World War I. It set a limit of 100,000 men with 5,000 officers for the German army and forbade the use of tanks, aircraft, submarines, and heavy

---

[24] Murray and Millett, 2

artillery. As a result, the military was denied access to crucial weapons emerging from the war. To compensate for these shortfalls, the German army took a systematic, holistic approach to examining the organizational, tactical, and technical lessons learn of that war and from that analysis created a very effective and comprehensive doctrine of combined arms and dominant maneuver. This became the foundation of the blitzkrieg tactics deployed by the German army during World War II. The Germans spent the entire decade thinking about warfare, technology, and arming their nation to fight the next war. The final product emphasized decentralized leadership and strict training and clearly demonstrated the Germans understood the nature of modern warfare.

This concept of fighting was developed without possessing a single tank, very limited knowledge on developing a mechanized, combined arms force, and without access to petroleum during the early stages of rearmament. The nearest major source was Romania, and the Romanians, along with the Czechs and Poles, were hostile to the Germans.

Germany's 1940 campaign was one of the most devastating, one-sided victories in the history of warfare. The French could not adapt to the tempo of this new combined arms technique. The glue that held the German forces together was a doctrine emphasizing speed, decentralized mission-type orders, decentralized command and control, and rapid exploitation of opportunities.

A couple things standout about the German transformation: (1) at the end of WW I, Germany was a vanquished nation so they began transforming their military with a clean slate. This allowed the Germans to develop their doctrine first and then match equipment to this doctrine; (2) their doctrine was based on a combined arms process utilizing army and air forces; (3) only those air and ground forces designed to "kick the door down" were transformed. The Germans, because their country stood in the center of Europe, had hostile neighbors to the east and west of its borders. As such, its concept of air operations was based in terms of Central European distances.[25] The end result was Germany, particularly in the opening weeks of World War II, had to support the army due to its poor geographical position.[26] (4) their methodology was effects based. The effect they were looking for was shock. Dive bombers were used to get this effect. The sight and sound of fighters raining bombs and bullets unto the field of battle was quite unnerving.

Carrier Aviation

Aircraft carrier development in the interwar era reflected the influence of strategic calculations. The United States and Japan envisioned a naval war fought in the Central Pacific where land-based air would be scarce and bases vulnerable. Britain, the third of the great carrier aviation pioneers, did not have the same compelling rationale for investment in carriers for many reasons: 1) the lack of an enemy carrier-based naval air threat in Europe; 2) the presumed availability of land-based air for maritime missions; and 3) the requirement for large surface forces to control the

---

[25] Ibid, 109.
[26] Ibid, 132.

approaches to the British Isles and the exits from the Baltic, the English Channel, and the Mediterranean. British naval planners, in addition, avoided shaping the Royal Navy for battle against one specific foe; instead, they followed a generalized theory of sea control, which tended to keep the Royal Navy rooted in its battleship past.[27] At the end of World War I, Britain was the only country possessing aircraft carriers. By 1939 Britain was surpassed by the American and Japanese carrier fleets.

Langley in Panama Canal

The U.S. Navy mastered the art of experimentation developing the carrier group concept. Test conducted at the Naval War College were unconstrained and had a high degree of realism. The necessity of massing aircraft for strikes was highlighted. Rather than assigning aircraft to each battleship to act as eyes, they were launched

---

[27] Ibid., 337

and kept in the air until large numbers could be assembled for an independent strike. Control of the air became the first goal of operations."[28]

For the British, their course of action was less clear because of uncertainty. Because of budget constraints and a political decision to limit military acquisition based on threat analysis in 1919, the British had no large battleship hull to convert. Instead, they used cruisers which had limited aircraft capacities. Under this scenario, it appeared it would be difficult to generate the number of aircraft necessary sink a properly supported battleship so the Royal Navy decided to make battleships the center of their service vice carriers.

"The most severe criticism that one can legitimately make about the Admiralty's carrier construction program is that it adopted a policy of excessive gradualism. In the early 1920s many design issues were unresolved. These included the development and positioning of arrester wires, catapults, carrier islands and included questions of the optimum size of carriers, whether they should be specialized or general purpose, and so on. On many matters, the British consciously and deliberately adopted a policy of 'waiting to see' or of leaving it to the Americans and Japanese to set the pace in such incremental innovation. The conscious decision to move slowly on the development of arrester wires and catapults, for example, was a serious mistake that considerably reduced the carrying capacity of British aircraft carriers, the size of the Fleet Air Arm, and the potential of both."[29]

---

[28] Steven Peter Rosen. *Winning the Next War, Innovation and the Modern Military* (Ithaca: Cornell University Press, 1991), 69.
[29] Murray and Millett, 198-199.

Lessons Learned From the Interwar Period

There are eight important lessons to be gained from the interwar period that are relevant to today's thinking about RMAs. What they reveal is a complex pattern of interactions between strategic assumptions, technological innovations, experimentation, doctrine, and civil-military relationships. The eight lessons are listed below:

RMAs are a crapshoot...there's nothing inevitable about their outcome

The German Army set out to build upon the operational and the tactical lessons learned of the First World War not create a new way of fighting. By reviewing the experiences of the last war with an open mind and examining that experience realistically, they moved, in fits and starts, toward developing a new concept of fighting.

Technology has only played a small part in past RMAs

Many of the key systems underlying the Blitzkrieg concept were already used in combat decades before the RMA occurred. Tanks, radios, and close air support aircraft were used in World War I, but they did not realize their true potential until the Germans devised new organizational and operational concepts for them in the 1930s. "What mattered most was that the Germans had evolved sound concepts for mobile, combined-arms warfare and had trained their army to execute those concepts."[30]

Success is the result of serious intellectual effort

The Germans put a premium not only on military readiness, but also on codifying military thought.

Honest historical analysis and experimentation can make or break an RMA

"The U.S. Navy's approach to war gaming was similar to that of the German Army. Neither military force used exercises or war gaming as a device to justify current, 'revealed' doctrine or as a means to exclude possibilities. In other

---

[30] Ibid, 373

words, exercises were aimed at illuminating possible uses for military forces and at suggesting what questions one might ask; they did not aim at providing 'solutions' or answers."[31]

Civilian and military leaders must be on the same page

There were four defining events in the development of American carrier aviation all tied to civilian and military leaders working toward a common goal. 1) key individuals such as William Sims and Admiral William Moffett attained bureaucratic positions from which they promoted and influenced development of naval aviation; 2) aviation emerged as a recognized and separately funded enterprise within the Department of the Navy thanks to civilian leaders; 3) changes in the external environment modified development of U.S. naval aviation; and 4) an ad hoc institutional process emerged for answering both conceptual and technical questions about how best to proceed in developing carriers and carrier aircraft at the insistence of Admiral Moffett.[32]

There must be a vision for the future

The evidence points, first of all, to the importance of developing visions of the future. The German's development of Blitzkrieg during the interwar period was structured on the broader aim of developing mobile warfare with the strategic context of a continental power potentially facing adversaries on two fronts.[33]

The presence of a specific problem to solve aids innovation

America's ability to point at the Japanese as a potential opponent was a tremendous asset in developing carrier aviation. It provided a criterion against which the U.S. Navy could judge their tactics and equipment. Without friendly local air power in support, the U.S. Navy would clearly have to take its own. Either to relieve the Philippines from a Japanese siege or, from the mid-1930s, to recapture them, the Americans expected to move westward across the Pacific without relying on bases in the theater and against a determined adversary.[34] The British, lacking this perspective, never felt a sense of urgency to develop carrier aviation.

Service culture can impact innovation

The development of the Blitzkrieg concept was marked by extremely high degrees cooperation between the army and air forces. This cooperation allowed

---

[31] Ibid., 317.
[32] Ibid., 392.
[33] Ibid, 407
[34] Ibid, 203.

the German military to perfect its combined arms concept of operation.

ASSESSMENT OF AIR FORCE TRANSFORMATION

Based upon the history of past RMAs, there appear to be missing elements in the Air Force's current goal to create an RMA (see Table 3). All successful RMAs driven by technology have three common components: transformational technologies; doctrine describing how to employ this new technology; and a military force structure specifically crafted to exploit the transformational technologies and new doctrine. Currently, there are three barriers the Air Force must clear to produce an RMA; joint doctrine, simulation and experimentation shortfalls, and service culture.

INTERWAR RMA CHECKLIST	CURRENT SITUATION
Transformational technologies	We clearly have this
Dynamic experimentation process	This seems to be missing
Receptive service culture	This could be a problem
Specific military problem to solve	Provided by QDR
Vision of the future	Missing coherent joint doctrine
Support from the top	We have this

Table 3: Interwar RMA Checklist

Barriers To Transformation

Joint Warfare Doctrine

Any Air Force which does not keep its doctrines ahead of its equipment, and its vision far into the future, can only delude the nation into a false sense of security.

-General Henry H. "Hap" Arnold

A dangerous vacuum exists today with our joint warfighting concepts. Military history since the outbreak of World War II has underscored the critical role of joint warfare. If the Armed Forces of today are to fully integrate and use the advanced weaponry of today, they must foster authentic jointness through doctrine and a common concept of operations.

Joint operations will be key in executing future defense strategies and missions. In modern warfare, each service requires contributions from the others in order to carry out it missions. Naval and marine amphibious forces are critical to securing access to littoral areas so as to allow ground and air forces to deploy safely. They also provide fully one-third of U.S. tactical air power and deep-strike assets for intense combat once deployment is complete. Ground forces require help from air power to degrade enemy maneuver forces and logistics support, while air forces benefit when ground forces compel the enemy to mass its forces, thereby exposing them to air attack.[35]

Operation Allied Force exposed holes in our current joint doctrine. The air war over Serbia identified the need to develop doctrine for contingencies in which the air

---

[35] Hans Binnendijk, *Transforming America's* Military (Washington DC: Defense University Press, 2002), 80.

component is the supported force and has been assigned missions and tasks normally associated with land forces. Although this is an air versus land example similar disconnects could occur with naval or Marine Corps functions. Joint doctrine should provide insight into such operations and clarify the roles of the participants.

Joint warfighting must be grounded in concepts that can provide flexibility of mind and habit. This is why we need a standing joint task force (SJTF) to develop a common operation plan for America's armed forces. The basis of a joint approach to operations is understanding each other's business. Officers must understand the core function of their service along with those of the sister services. Also, competing military theories of fighting require exploration and analysis at the tactical level of war so decision makers can have a true sense of their viability and implementation.

"The QDR specifically mandate the creation of a standing joint task force concept of operations for unwarned, extended-range conventional attack against fixed and mobile targets at any range. The concept, unnamed in the QDR but informally known as 'Stealth Task Force' or 'Global Surveillance Strike' is designed to support the key DoD transformation goal of denying enemies the sanctuary through persistent surveillance, tracking, and rapid engagement. The QDR cited this particular joint power projection concept as having the potential to become the vanguard of U.S. military transformation."[36]

Each of the services has developed warfighting concepts which could serve as the underpinnings of a joint warfighting architecture. Of the joint strike CONOPs proposed

---

[36] General Richard E. Hawley (USAF-Ret) and others, "Enhancing USAF's Pacific Posture: How The Air Force Can Transform To Support A New Joint Warfighting Architecture," *Armed Forces Journal*, September 2002, 55.

by services, Global Strike Task Force (GSTF) in the Air Force, Expeditionary Strike Groups (ESGs) under the Navy/Marine Corps team, and Striker Brigades within the Army, the Global Strike Task Force is furthest along. GSTF incorporates many of the network centric battle management concepts espoused by the Navy and relies on joint fires to shape the battlefield. Although air and space centric, the concept foresees ground forces playing an integral role in finding and fixing forces during joint fire sessions.[37]

Simulation and Experimentation

Institutional processes for exploring, testing, and refining conceptions of future war are literally the sine qua non of successful military innovation in peacetime.

-Barry Watts and Williamson Murray
Military Innovation in the Interwar Period

The modern use of simulations and war games has its roots in the numerous exercises the Department of the United States Navy conduct during the interwar period between WWI and WWII to flush out doctrine and best practices for carrier aviation. The history of war gaming is imbedded in the Navy. The Joint Staff must emulate this spirit and create its own identity in pushing modern warfare to the next level.

Uncertainty about future threats requires an approach that manages uncertainty through war games and simulations designed to explore the shape of potential wars. The ambiguous costs and benefits of new tools and tactics can only be explored

---

[37] Ibid, 55.

through critical evaluations designed to highlight learn from mistakes.[38] The German Army and U.S. Navy applied this approach during the interwar period when developing blitzkrieg tactics and carrier aviation. Both are examples of successful peacetime transformations and both illustrate the impact candid exercises and thorough assessments can have on the transformation process. When assessments validate an idea, support grows, and when they uncover faults, refinements can be made to strengthen a concept or scrap the idea completely.

Though it was instituted in October 1999 to stimulate military transformation, the experimentation mission of U.S. Joint Forces Command has neither the authority nor the resources to accomplish that risk. It can lead only when the services have no interests at stake. Moreover, the experimentation is funded at a level below that needed to gauge the best ways to capitalize on technology. Experiments tend to look at ways of modifying current procedures.

Service Culture

New technologies will increasingly bring to fore the expert in missile operations, the space genera, and the electronic warfare wizard...none of them a combat specialist in the old sense
-Eliot Cohen, A Revolution in Warfare

Culture is the system of underlying, shared beliefs about the critical tasks and relationships within an organization. Organizations will resist taking on new tasks that

---

[38] "National Security Strategy in the 21st Century: The Challenge of Transformation," Joint Force Quarterly, Summer 1997, 15-19

are incompatible with their dominant culture.[39]

The revolution that's underway is being dominated by the emergence of precision weapons along with the coupled with sensors. What's missing are those innovations which take the human element out of war, often the weakest link. The services seem hesitant push the advances of robotics and unmanned vehicles. Unmanned vehicles are being deployed today but with limited combat capability and we have yet to see similar devices for underwater or urban environments.

One area where these technologies would be of great use is in engaging elusive moving ground threats. Striking mobile targets such as ballistic missile launchers has persisted as a problem area for planners. These targets often manage to escape an area by the time intelligence assets have detected and targeted the systems. They could provide an entirely different way of engaging an enemy. They could monitor an area, and when a target appears, strike immediately using onboard computer or when

---

[39] Edgar H. Schein, *The Corporate Culture Survival Guide: Sense and Nonsense About Culture Change* (San Francisco, CA: Josey-Bass Publishers, 1999), 186.

commanded by remote operator. This approach could be considered an asymmetric approach to killing the enemy.

UAV type programs have not fared well in the past. UAV programs like Global Hawk and Predator were forced on a reluctant Air Force. Yet, the service has prospered because of their operational usefulness, as demonstrated in combat. If the Air Force was forced to utilize useful systems such as these, what will the future hold?

Unmanned aerial vehicles should be a growth industry for the United States armed forces. In the end, what it takes to win wars is firepower, firepower that has been massed for maximum effects. UAVs can provide these massed effects. We need to pursue technology that puts steel on targets at minimum risk to personnel. When we start fielding and employing UAVs in formations normally associated with combat squadrons and wings, we can really start talking about the revolutionary affects of technology. Global Hawk and Predator bring persistence and endurance to the fight and have the potential to make their mark against high risk targets we wouldn't normally send aircrews against until late in the fight after the enemy has been shaped.

The last fighter pilot may not have been born, but the last fighter pilot flying over Baghdad or any other area saturated with counter-air defenses may have been born. That role should go to UAVs. That should be our future along with technologies in robotics, nanotechnology, and biotechnology. War is a human endeavor, you can never take men completely out of the loop, but you can reduce the impact of this weak link in combat systems, especially in revolving around large scale contingencies.

CONCLUSION

This paper set out to answer two fundamental questions. First, are the F/A-22, Space Based Radar, and Small Diameter Bomb, transformational technologies? Second, if they are transformational technologies, will they lead to a revolution in military affairs?

Transformation is such an enormous issue because it is concerned with preparing for the future. Transformations represent a series of evolutionary changes in technology, organizations, and concepts of operation. Transformation can involve several aspects: armed forces can invent a new capability, a leap-ahead technology, or they can make a current capability exponentially better. Transformations are a necessary precursor in the process of achieving a revolution in military affairs. It is the synergistic affect of combining transformational changes in the above mentioned elements which leads to revolutions in military affairs.

The F/A-22 and Small Diameter Bomb are transformational technologies. Each represents evolutionary steps forward for the respective systems they will replace or complement in the future. It's too early to determine the disposition of the Spaced Based Radar because its final architecture has not been determined. While each technology should make considerable contributions to future warfare, they do not come without a cost, namely, they could hurt long term national security interests by diverting funding from critical requirements such as manpower, installations, and other combat, space, and mobility systems.

The current period of transformation is analogous to the interwar period of the 1920s and 1930s. That was an era where threats were uncertain, technological changes were occurring at a rapid pace, and defense resources were limited. What occurred during this period was a series of revolutions in military affairs. Military organizations matched technological changes with new doctrines and operational concepts. The resultant efforts were carrier aviation and the blitzkrieg concept.

It's too early to tell whether development of the F/A-22, SBR, and SDB will lead to a RMA. This current period of change is missing several elements essential to cultivating a RMA. They include: shortfalls in joint doctrine, parochial service cultures, and limited simulation and experimentation. None of these issues are insurmountable. The services must seriously address joint warfare doctrine, as all future conflicts will be fought under a joint/combined arms concept. No single service has the means to win a major theater war single-handedly. The lack of a clear statement outlining how services intend to fight and what services anticipate is required for success in joint operations obstructs any real promise of Department of Defense transformation and the potential for entering a revolution in military affairs. We must come to grips with an appropriate ethos for our service cultures. Our warrior values play a significant role in the inability of the services to finalize a joint warfighting document and in determining the appropriate force structure for future, jointly fought wars. Even if we fix joint doctrine and quell the force of service culture, current war gaming capabilities are inadequate. War gaming was a vital element in developing new operational concepts during the interwar period. To bring about a RMA, we must have mechanisms in place to allow services to experiment with new ideas of joint warfighting. This will the services to discover what they can do with new technologies in a joint environment, what existing military tasks can be done differently, and finally make honest decisions on what works and what doesn't work. If the services can clear these hurdles, they may well be on their way to a RMA.

BIBLIOGRAPHY

Schneider, Barry R. and Lawrence E. Grinter. *Battlefield of the Future: 21st Century Warfare Issues*. Maxwell Air Force Base, AL: Air University Press, 1998.

Melinger, Philip S. *The Paths of Heaven – The Evolution of Airpower Theory*. Maxwell Air Force Base, AL: Air University Press, 2001.

Mets, David R. *The Long Search for a Surgical Strike: Precision Munitions and the Revolution in Military Affairs*. Maxwell Air Force Base, AL: Air University Press, 2001.

HQ USAF/XPXT. *The USAF Transformation Flight Plan FY03-07*. United States Air Force Transformation Division, 2002.

HQ ACC/DR. *CAF Operational Requirements Document for Miniature Munitions and Carriage System*.

Alberts, David S., John J. Garstka, and Fredrick P. Stein. *Network Centric Warfare: Developing and Leveraging Information Superiority*. C4ISR Cooperative Research Program, 2000.

Transforming America's Military. Ed. Hans Binnendijk. Washington, D.C.: National Defense University Press, 2002.

Vick, Alan, and others. *Aerospace Operations Against Elusive Ground Targets*. Santa Monica, CA: RAND, 2001.

Hura, Myron, and others. *Enhancing Dynamic Command and Control of Air Operations Against Time Critical Targets*. Santa Monica, CA: RAND, 2002.

Vega, Milan. "Net-Centric Is Not Decisive.", *Proceedings*, January 2003.

Barnett, Jeffery R. *Future War: An Assessment of Aerospace Campaigns in 2010.*
    Maxwell Air Force Base, AL: Air University Press, 1996.

Parker, Geoffrey. *The Military Revolution: Military Innovation and the Rise of the West,*
    1500-1800. Cambridge, UK: Cambridge University Press, 1996.

Department of Defense, "Quadrennial Defense Review." 2001

Krepinevich, Andrew. "Transforming the American Military." *Backgrounder*, 26
    September 1997.

Kingdom of Sweden, *Annual Exchange of Information on Defense Planning*, Vienna
    Document 1999.

Bush, George W., President. Speech presented at the National Defense University,
    Washington, DC, 2001.

Tirpak, John A. "The Space Based Radar Plan." *Air Force Magazine*, August 2002.

Scott, William B. "Innovation Is Currency of USAF Space Battlelab," *Aviation Week and*
    Space Technology, 3 April 2000, 52-53.

Murray, William and Allan R. Millett, *Military Innovation in the Interwar Period.* New
    York, NY: Cambridge University Press, 1996.

Simpson, Randall. "Transforming Explosive Art Into Science," www.llnl.gov/html.

Hawley, General Richard E. (USAF-Ret) and others. "Enhancing USAF's Pacific
    Posture: How The Air Force Can Transform To Support A New Joint Warfighting
    Architecture." *Armed Forces Journal*, September 2002, 54-61.

Schein, Edgar H. *The Corporate Culture Survival Guide: Sense and Nonsense About Culture Change.* San Francisco: Josey-Bass Publishers, 1999.